I0199266

THE GIRL WHO TURNS INTO A TREE

by
Linda C. Ehrlich

Images by
Antonia Cruz, Pamela McKee and Susan Griffith

Layout designed by
Jared Bendis

The Girl Who Turns Into a Tree
by Linda C. Ehrlich

Copyright © 2016 by Shika Press LTD

All rights reserved.

ISBN - 978-0-9858786-7-2

Published by Shika Press LLC

Shika Press Ltd.

Shaker Heights, Ohio, USA

This book is dedicated to all those who work for the dignity and education of young women.

In an ancient Greek myth, the nymph Daphne, daughter of the River god Peneus, is used as a pawn by the trickster god of Love, Cupid, as part of Cupid's revenge for the way Apollo, the Sun god, had mocked him. Cupid shoots a leaden arrow of hatred into Daphne but a golden arrow of desire into Apollo. Pursued by Apollo against her will, Daphne pleads to her father to save her by transforming her form into a tree…

ROOTS

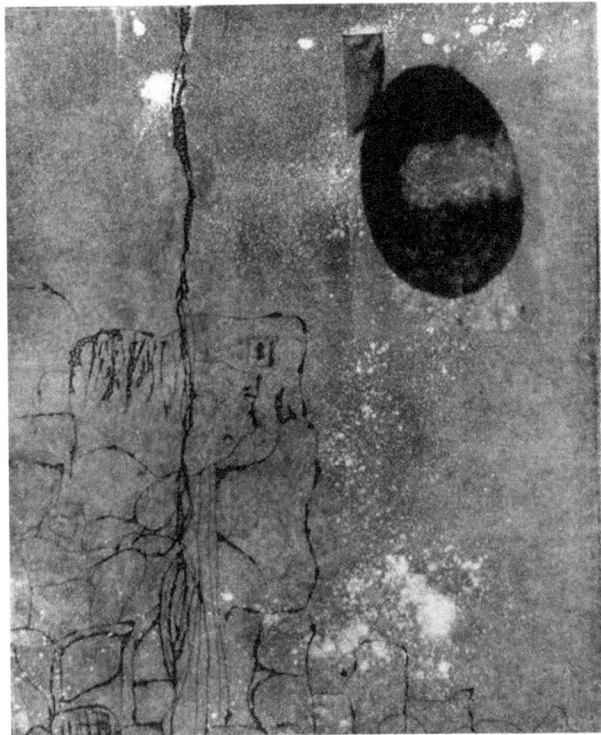

Red roots
Yellow branches

the weaving and unweaving of light.

Marble light
climbs
terraced hillsides,

across a frieze of charioteers.

She dreams a dream of a girl
in a distant land who has turned into a tree,

her narrow roots clutching the soil.

Glossy leaves
soft
and evergreen,

almost illegible.

Her canopy,
the turquoise sky.

Earth beneath the bones of her feet
still warm.

I have heard tales…

At sunset the sky turns a crystal blue
and gold leaks into the water.

As a young girl swinging from branches,
never imagining
such a fate.

Apollo, the metal arrow of love,
Daphne, the leaden arrow of hatred.

Beneath his balcony…

Running
First her arms become quivering branches.

Each golden strand of her hair,
an almond-shaped leaf.

Terror awakens in the night.

From a distance no one sees the scars. Cracked. Her face is cracked like a porcelain doll dropped on the pavement. Young skin cracked open. The damage years.

Daphne must choose. Open up to the sky, or be captured.

Green eyes,

Green heart.

She has come to the gathering point.
Gathering and discarding.

New growth sprouts
from her outstretched fingers.

In the faint whisper of the wind
she can hear the sound
of her name
returning.

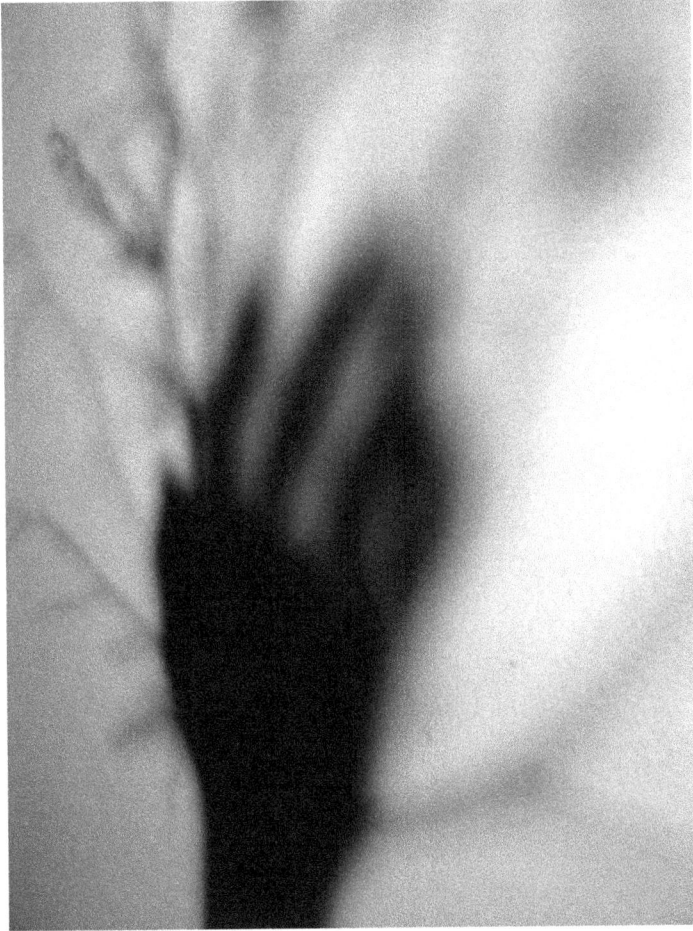

BRANCHES

Not the whispering acacia with its bitter bark
nor the miniature cypress, pillar of flame,
        guarding the cemeteries.

Not the aged olive
with its stubborn fruit,
nor the carob with its raucous skin and dangling tresses.

A laurel
wrapped in oval leaves
Silent
but for the wind.

Now certain that the sky is only the sky, never closer,

The Earth, only the earth—at times firm, at times shifting,
she saw,
immobile
no longer running,
no longer fleeing from what falls away at her feet.

The cool of the orchard with its promises:
juniper's
healing balm.

Whatever you are forced to be—

    shadows, mirrors, empty pools—

Imagine yourself rooted
Verdant.

A golden tree
cleansing the air.

LEAVES

Solitary
but not alone.

Ancestors tendril around you.

Apollo
no longer the unwitting hunter.

A river
cooling roots,

branches,

leaves.

Now your body
Remembers

    ample

               Oracles of light.

Illustrations

Figure and Ground I, 2015, photogram (Photograph courtesy of Antonia Cruz) – cover & page 37

The abstract designs for Roots (page 5), Branches (page 17), & Leaves (page 23) chapter divisions are by Cleveland artist Pamela McKee who works in Japanese *shibori*, collage, and fish prints.

Apollo and Daphne, Massimilliano Soldani, c. 1700. (Cleveland Museum of Art. Photograph courtesy of Corey Wright.) – page 10

Ana Josefa, 2011, digital photomontage (Photograph courtesy of Antonia Cruz) – page 12

Change (Photograph courtesy of Susan Griffith) – page 15

Water Picture, Horseshoe Lake (Photograph courtesy of Susan Griffith) – page 21

Figure and Ground II, 2015, photogram (Photograph courtesy of Antonia Cruz) – page 25

Reflection in Water, Shaker Lakes (Photograph courtesy of Susan Griffith) – page 27

With thanks to Rhina Espaillat for her comments on a draft of this writing.

Contributors

Antonia Cruz
Antonia Cruz Subercaseaux, visual artista (b. Santiago, Chile,1984). In 2009 Cruz received her Bachelor's degree in Visual Arts from Finis Terrae University, Santiago, Chile. In 2010 she studied photography with Enrique Zamudio, within the framework of the Graduate Program in Photography at Finis Terrae, and during 2011 she was educated in Anatomical Techniques and Conservation Methods in the Morphology Program at the University of Chile Medicine Faculty, Santiago. Solo exhibitions of her work have been held in Milan, Santiago, and Cleveland. She has also exhibited in group shows in Kochi (India), Berlin, Lima (Peru), Lodz (Poland), Barcelona, and Porto Alegre (Brazil).

"*Figure and Ground* is made from large-scale photograms of silhouettes of the artist as another. One figure confronts and is incorporated into the landscape (drawn from negatives of U.S. locales in the 1920s)."

Pamela McKee
Cleveland Heights-based artist Pamela McKee has been influenced by the *shibori* work of Yoshiko Wada and Joan Morris, and inspired by the work of Dutch artist Marian Bijlenga. She has an MA in English literature and taught English for 25 years, while taking art classes, attending workshops, and developing her art. She has attended Haystack Mountain School of Crafts, Penland School of Crafts, Arrowmont School of Arts and Crafts, and has taken art classes at the Cleveland Institute of Art, Cuyahoga Community College, and the Morgan Art of Papermaking Conservatory.

Susan B. Griffith

Griffith's photographic montages have appeared in numerous gallery shows and magazines, such as *Black and White Magazine, Color, F-Stop Magazine,* and the launch issue of *Focus Folios* (20 pages of images). Her work has received international recognition as finalists in the Sixth and Seventh Julia Margaret Cameron Award for Women Photographers, with "Bird Story" among the selected few finalists exhibited at the Heritage Museum in Málaga, Spain in 2014. It was also part of a portfolio that received first place in TBM's portfolio competition in 2013. Her photograph of "Flight: Inspired by Carol Holmes" appears on the cover of Ehrlich's *In the Breathing Time.*

Corey Wright

Corey Wright holds a dual degree in Mechanical and Aerospace Engineering from Case Western Reserve University as well as a Master of Engineering and Management degree from Case's Weatherhead School of Management. He is Founder & CEO of Technically Wright Consulting where he helps local residents and small businesses find creative technology solutions.

Jared Bendis

Jared Bendis is the Creative New Media Officer for Case Western Reserve University's Kelvin Smith Library. He is also an installation artist, photographer, teacher, playwright, and filmmaker. Bendis has designed all of Ehrlich's books of poetry, and also *Good Films, Cheap Wine, Few Friends: A Memoir* by Juan Luis Buñuel (edited and annotated by L. Ehrlich).

Linda Ehrlich

Linda Ehrlich's writing has been described as "haunting, exquisitely sensitive." She has published poetry in *International Poetry Review, Southern Poetry Review, The Bitter Oleander, Literary Arts Hawaii, Puppetry International*, and several literary journals in Spain and Japan. Her poetry and prose poetry have been gathered into three richly illustrated anthologies published by Shika Press: *In the Breathing Time, Night Harbour,* and *Bodegón/Still Life,* and one book on world dance for young readers *The Body is Round.*

For more information, please note the website: http://braidednarrative.com

The Girl who Turns into a Tree was inspired by my hope that young women will maintain faith in their abilities, despite obstacles placed in their path.

www.ingramcontent.com/pod-product-compliance
Lightning Source LLC
Chambersburg PA
CBHW040245100426

42811CB00011B/1156